I0148885

I Want to Learn
al-Ikhlaas al-Falaq an-Nas

Written by Umm Bilaal Bint Sabir
Content Review @utrujjah_press
Cover Formatting @ilm.cards
Proofreading Umm AbdurRahmaan S. Bint Ahmed and Umm Yunus
Typesetting by Umm Bilaal Bint Sabir

2023 Al Huroof Publishing
© alhuroof
First Published August 2024

ISBN 978-1-917065-22-1

All rights reserved. No part of this publication may be reproduced stored in a retrieval system or transmitted in any form or by any means electronic, mechanical, photocopying, recording or otherwise without the prior written permission of the author.

All enquiries to: alhuroof@hotmail.com
@al.huroof

Al Huroof Publishing

Learning my 1st Short Surahs

This book belongs to:

Dedicated to Ahsan,
Allaah yarhamhu, a special boy who taught
the author the last two surahs of the Qur'aan,
in his short but blessed life.

May Allaah Subhanahu, increase his
reward of sadaqa jariyah ameen.

بسم الله

All Praise is for Allaah the Lord of the whole of creation and may Allaah extol and grant peace and security to our Prophet Muhammad (sallAllaahu 'alayhi wa sallam), and to his true followers and to his companions (radhiAllaahu 'anhum), all of them.

To Proceed:

How to Use this Book

Learning to read the Qur'aan is a difficult task for non-Arab speakers, especially if you are not familiar with the letters (huroof), sounds (tajweed) and vowels (harakaat) of the Arabic language. This book has been designed as a temporary helping guide for English Speakers who need help in the beginning to understand how to pronounce the Arabic sounds.

We have included the Arabic, the English transliteration and the translation to help you pronounce the letters. We have also added a short explanation of each ayah, although there is much more to learn about these beautiful short surahs. The translation has been taken from The Noble Qur'aan, Darussalaam by Dr. Muhammad Hilali and Dr.Muhsin Khan.

The best way to learn the Qur'aan

The best way to learn the Qur'aan is to find a Qur'aan teacher who can teach you in Arabic. This is the best and blessed way to learn.

This book is just a temporary guide until you find someone who can teach you how to recite properly.

About Al Huroof
Al Huroof is a small project aimed at producing authentic Islamic teaching aids and material. These are based on the Qur'aan and Sunnah, with the understanding of the Prophet Muhammad (sallAllaahu 'alayhi wa sallam), and his righteous companions - Salaf-us-Saalih - (radhiAllaahu 'anhum). After thanking Allaah, Subhaanahu, we would like to thank all those who have aided in this book, from formatting, checking and feedback.

May Allaah accept it as sadaqa jaariyah from us, ameen.

4

I want to learn

Surah
al-Ikhlaas
al-Falaq
an-Nas

How do I start?

Let's go over some basic Arabic vowels that you will need for these suwar.

Each ayah (verse) has been divided word by word. When you see this little sign it means 'Iqra' (read or recite).

Tafsīrāt of these suwar are taken from At-Tabari, Imam as Sa'di, Sahih al-Bukhari rahimahumallaah and others. These have been explained by Shaykh Uthaymeen rahimahullah and Shaykh Fawzaan hafidhahullaah.

اقرأ

Basic Vowels

Dhamma
وُ بُ اُ
tu bu 'u

Kasrah
تِ بِ اِ
ti bi ii

Fathah
تَ بَ اَ
ta ba a

Shaddah
بُّ اَ   بِّ اَ   بَّ اَ
ab-bu   ab-bi   ab-ba

Sukoon
بْ اُ   بْ اِ   بْ اَ
ub   ib   ab

Dhammatayn
بٌ اٌ
bunn unn

Kasrahtayn
بٍ اٍ
binn inn

Fatahtayn
بًا اً
bann ann

Lam - alif
لاَ لا
laa

Hamza-alif
اُ اِ اَ
'u 'i 'a

Madd
الضَّالِّينَ
4 or 6 counts

Dagger Alif
الرَّحْمٰنُ
This is a long 'a' sound

Hamza-tul Wasl
ا
This sound is not said if connecting with a previous word.

7

Bismillaah

In the Name of Allaah

We say bismillaah before we recite the Quraan.

We also say it before we do something so that we can get Allaah's help and blessings in what we do.

Saying bismillaah means we are calling upon all the names of Allaah.

بِسْمِ اللَّهِ

اقرأ

ar-Rahmaan

The Most Merciful

This is one of the beautiful names of Allaah.
It means 'Rahma' which is mercy.
Allaah has a vast amount of Mercy and is the Most Merciful to all of His creation. We receive His Mercy everyday in so many ways.

الرَّحْمَنِ

اقرأ

ar-Raheem

The Ever-Merciful

This is another one of the beautiful names of Allaah.

It means He is more Merciful, and gives special Mercy to those who believe in Him, those who follow His Prophets and His Messengers; and are Muslims.

الرَّحِيمِ

اقرأ

now say it together

Bismillaahir

Rahmaanir Raheem

In the name of Allaah,
The Most Merciful,
The Ever-Merciful.

بِسْمِ اللّٰهِ الرَّحْمٰنِ الرَّحِيمِ

Qul huwa Allaahu Ahad

Say   **He is**   **Allaah**   **(who is) One**

The non-believers or Jews asked the Prophet (sallAllaahu 'alayhi wa sallam) to describe his God and what He is made of! So Allaah revealed this surah for the Prophet (sallAllaahu 'alayhi wa sallam) and all Muslims to say.

Allaah is The One.
He is Unique in His Glory.

He is the Almighty and the Only One.

He has no partner and there is no one like Him.

Musnad Ahmad, Ibn Kathir, Tirmidhi Tafsir

قُلْ هُوَ ٱللَّهُ أَحَدٌ

Allaahu-s Samad

Allaah is **The Self-Sufficient**

As-Samad is the Perfect Lord and Master.* He is the One who all His creatures need and are dependent on.

The One Who remains and never dies, the One Who neither eats nor drinks, free of all needs.

As-Samad means He is Complete in His Knowledge, Patience, Might and Ability.**

The One who is not in need of His creatures.

*The Ninety-Nine Names of Allaah – Dawud Burbank

**Al-'Aqidah Al-Wasitiyyah (2 Vol. Set) – Author: Shaykh Muhammad bin Salih Al-'Uthaimin – Publisher: Darussalam Publishers & Distributors

اَللَّهُ ٱلصَّمَدُ

Lam Yalid

He does not (beget) have children...

To beget means to have a child.
To have a child means you have a partner.

Allaah is free from this.
He does not beget because there
is no one like Him.
Allaah, the Almighty, the Glorious has
no need of a child or a partner.

How could He have a son
or partner when
He created everything?*

*Surah Al An'am ayat 101

لَمْ يَلِذْ

walam yulad

nor is He born

Allaah is the First. There is nothing before Him.*

He created everything. Nothing was before Him.

He created everything. How could He be born?

The non-believers say angels are
the daughters of Allaah!

The Jews say Uzair is the son of Allaah!

The Christians say Jesus
is the son of Allaah!**

None of them are true!

*The Ninety-Nine Names of Allaah – Dawud Burbank
Surah Maryam ayah 88

22

وَلَمْ يُولَدْ

now say it together

Lam Yalid walam yulad

He does not (beget) have children, nor is He born.

لَمْ يَلِدْ
وَلَمْ يُولَدْ

اقرأ

walam yaku-llahu

nor is   there   to Him

kufuwan ahad

anyone equal

There is no one equal to Him in His qualities.

Allaah denies that He begets or is born
or that anything is equal to Him.

وَلَمْ يَكُن لَّهُ كُفُوًا أَحَدٌ

Bismillaahir Rahmaanir Raheem

In the name of Allaah,
The Most Merciful,
The Ever-Merciful.

بِسْمِ اللّٰهِ الرَّحْمٰنِ الرَّحِيمِ

اقرأ

Qul 'authu dhu

Say: I seek refuge

bi Rabbi-l- falaq

with the Lord of the daybreak.

The Lord of the daybreak and dawn is
Allaah. Allaah brings out the dawn and
everything else that grows,
like grains, and fruit seeds that
split and sprout*

*Surah al-An'am ayat 95-96

قُلْ أَعُوذُ بِرَبِّ ٱلْفَلَقِ

min sharri maa khalaq

From the evil of what He has created.

This includes the evil of the creatures and the evil of ourselves. Why ourselves? Because we are part of the creation and our souls are created weak. We can go towards things that are wrong. So we seek refuge from our own souls first.*

We also seek refuge from the shaytaan, jinns, wild animals and everything else in the creation.

Khutabbal al Hajjar

مِن شَرِّ
مَا خَلَقَ

اقرأ

wa min sharri

And from the evil of
ghaasiqin itha waqab

the night when it grows dark.

This means when the night enters with its darkness it becomes Ghaasiq.* This is when wild animals and beasts come out. It also means when the moon brightens with its light. It is also Ghaasiq** because it only happens at night.

Allaah created the darkness, the night and everything in it and we seek refuge from the evil of it all.

*Surah Al-Isra ayah 78
Sunan al-Tirmidhī 3366

وَمِن شَرِّ غَاسِقٍ إِذَا وَقَبَ

اقرأ

35

wa min sharrin

↓ ↓ ↓

And from the evil of those

nafathaa ti fil ʿuqad

↓ ↓ ↓ ↓

who blow in the knots.

These are the evil witches who tie knots and make spells with the names of the shayateen when they blow onto the knots.
They tie and blow, tie and blow, tie and blow. They are wicked men or women who want to harm other people.

Allaah is the Only One to protect us.

وَمِن شَرِّ ٱلنَّفَّثَتِ فِى ٱلْعُقَدِ

اقرأ

wa min sharri

↓ ↓ ↓

And from the evil of the

haa sidin idhaa hasad

↓ ↓ ↓ ↓

envier when he envies

The envier is one who does not like to see people have blessings from Allaah.

They are upset to see what Allaah gives to others like money, honour, knowledge or even a nice car.

This is the evil eye. When a person or their things are harmed by others.

وَمِن شَرِّ حَاسِدٍ إِذَا حَسَدَ

اقرأ

now say it together

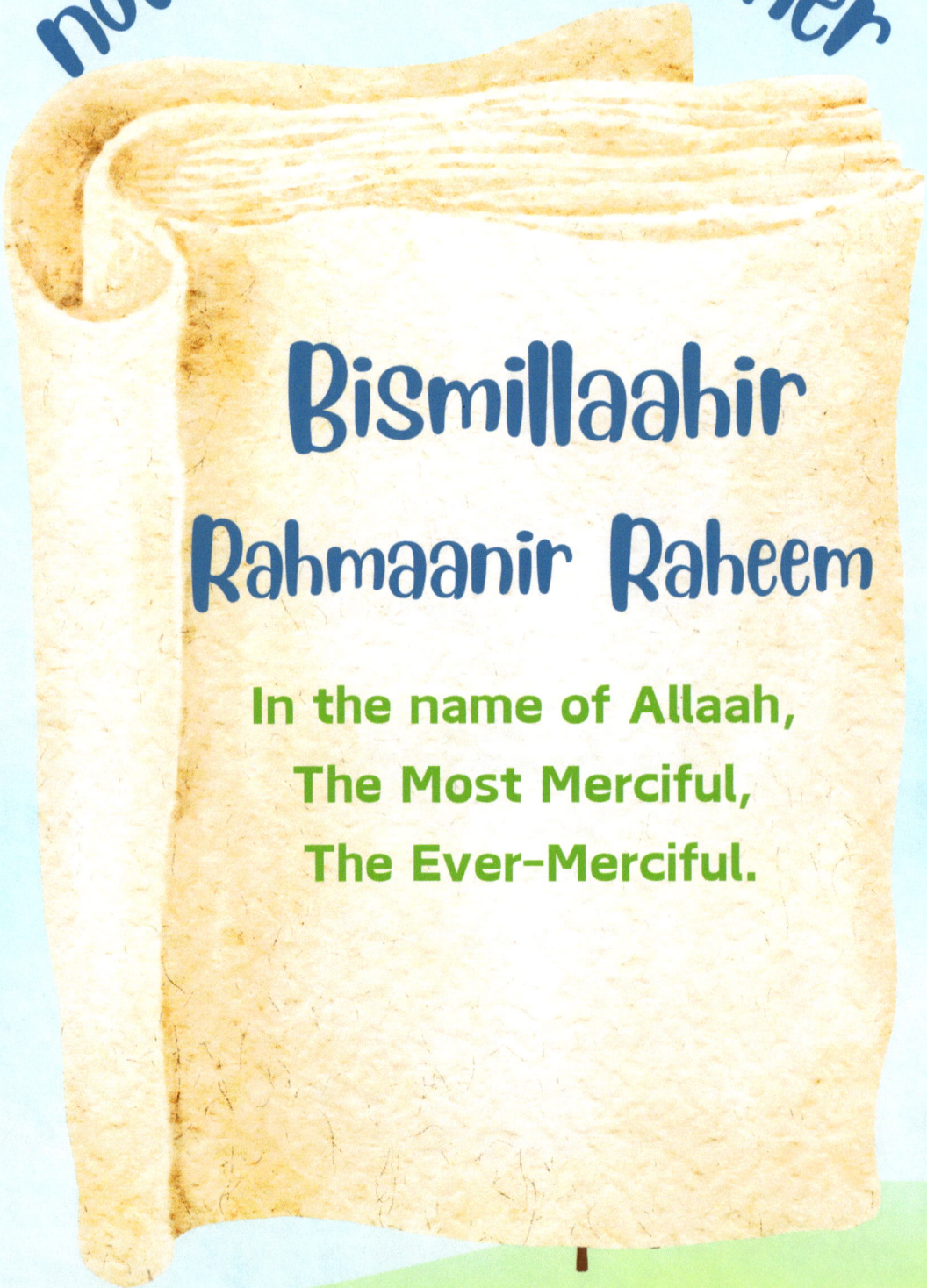

Bismillaahir Rahmaanir Raheem

**In the name of Allaah,
The Most Merciful,
The Ever-Merciful.**

بِسْمِ اللَّهِ أَلرَّحْمَٰنِ الرَّحِيمِ

اقرأ

Qul ʿAuthu

Say: I seek refuge

Allaah is telling the Prophet (sallAllaahu ʿalayhi wa salaam), and mankind to seek safety, refuge or shelter.

قُلْ أَعُوذُ

bi-Rabbi-ni-naas

⬇ ⬇ ⬇ ⬇

with the Lord of mankind.

Ar-Rabb is the Lord, who takes care of His slaves through His blessings on them. He guides them, gives them knowledge, provides for them and controls everything.

Ar-Rabb is the Lord of all the people, the angels and the jinn, the skies, the earth, the sun, the moon and all that exists.

Here Allaah only mentions people.

بِرَبِّ النَّاسِ

اقرأ

now say it together

Qul ʾAuthu bi-Rabbi-ni-naas

Say: I seek refuge with the Lord of mankind.

قُلْ أَعُوذُ بِرَبِّ النَّاسِ

اقْرَأْ

Maliki-n-naas

The King of mankind

The King of mankind who is the only One with the Almighty Power and Complete ownership over people. He is Allaah, the Almighty.

Allaah gives power to whom He wills, and takes it away from whom He wills, honours whom He wills and degrades who He wills ...*

Surah Al-'Imran ayah 26

مَلِكِ ٱلنَّاسِ

اقْرَأ

Ilaahi-n-naas

The Ilaah (God) of mankind,

The Ilaah of mankind means He is the Almighty and the Only one to be worshipped.

The Only One to be worshipped and praised in the hearts, is Allaah, The Mighty.

إِلَهِ ٱلنَّاسِ

اقرأ

min sharril

↓ ↓

From the evil of the

waswaasil khannas

↓ ↓

whisperer who withdraws

The whispers from shaytaan are ideas or thoughts that are not real.

Al-Khannas is the shaytaan who runs when the person remembers Allaah, and returns when they forget about Allaah.

He runs away so fast when he hears the athan and is so sad to hear the name of Allaah!

مِن شَرِّ ٱلْوَسْوَاسِ ٱلْخَنَّاسِ

اقرأ

53

alladhi yu waswisu

Who   whispers

fi Sudoorin-nas

in the breasts of mankind.

When shaytaan whispers into the hearts of people we should quickly turn to Allaah, the Perfect, the Most High.

Only by remembering Allaah can we be safe from these whispers.

ٱلَّذِى
يُوَسْوِسُ
فِى صُدُورِ
ٱلنَّاسِ

اقْرَأ

min al jinnati wannas

from   the   jinn   and mankind

This means that the whispers
from the jinn or mankind.

The whispers of jinn are well known,
because they flow in people like
blood in the veins.

The whispers are from people who
come with evil thoughts or ideas
and make them look beautiful –
until you follow them!
We ask Allaah to
protect us.

مِنَ ٱلْجِنَّةِ
وَٱلنَّاسِ

اقرأ

When you
are ready you
can try and
recite the suwar
together!

سُورَةُ الْإِخْلَاصِ

🩵 بِسْمِ ٱللَّهِ ٱلرَّحْمَٰنِ ٱلرَّحِيمِ

قُلْ هُوَ ٱللَّهُ أَحَدٌ ﴿١﴾ ٱللَّهُ ٱلصَّمَدُ ﴿٢﴾

لَمْ يَلِدْ وَلَمْ يُولَدْ ﴿٣﴾ وَلَمْ يَكُن لَّهُۥ كُفُوًا أَحَدٌۢ ﴿٤﴾

سُورَةُ الْفَلَقِ

🩵 بِسْمِ ٱللَّهِ ٱلرَّحْمَٰنِ ٱلرَّحِيمِ

قُلْ أَعُوذُ بِرَبِّ ٱلْفَلَقِ ﴿١﴾

مِن شَرِّ مَا خَلَقَ ﴿٢﴾ وَمِن شَرِّ غَاسِقٍ إِذَا وَقَبَ ﴿٣﴾

وَمِن شَرِّ ٱلنَّفَّٰثَٰتِ فِى ٱلْعُقَدِ ﴿٤﴾ وَمِن شَرِّ حَاسِدٍ إِذَا حَسَدَ ﴿٥﴾

سُورَةُ النَّاسِ

🩵 بِسْمِ ٱللَّهِ ٱلرَّحْمَٰنِ ٱلرَّحِيمِ

قُلْ أَعُوذُ بِرَبِّ ٱلنَّاسِ ﴿١﴾ مَلِكِ ٱلنَّاسِ ﴿٢﴾

إِلَٰهِ ٱلنَّاسِ ﴿٣﴾ مِن شَرِّ ٱلْوَسْوَاسِ ٱلْخَنَّاسِ ﴿٤﴾

ٱلَّذِى يُوَسْوِسُ فِى صُدُورِ ٱلنَّاسِ ﴿٥﴾ مِنَ ٱلْجِنَّةِ وَٱلنَّاسِ

Learning my 1st Short Surahs

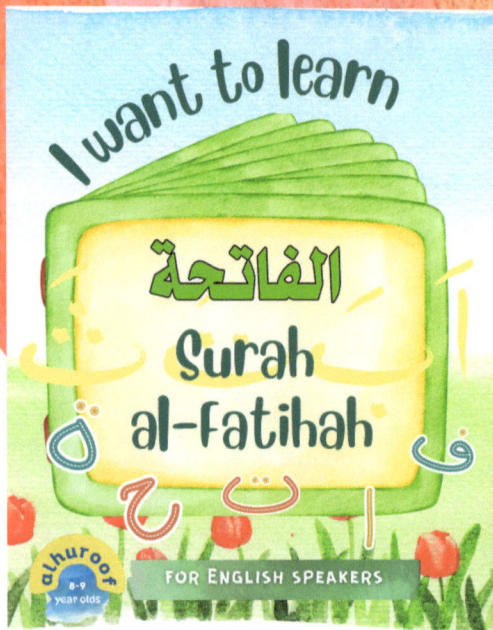

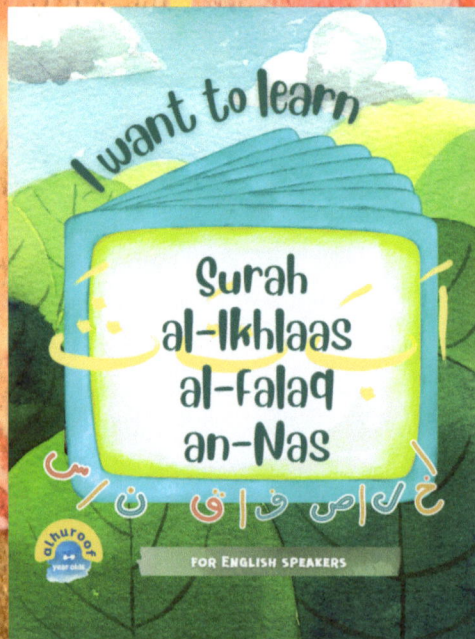

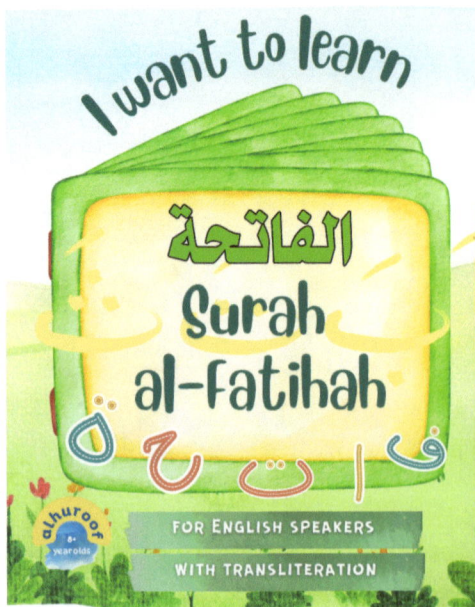

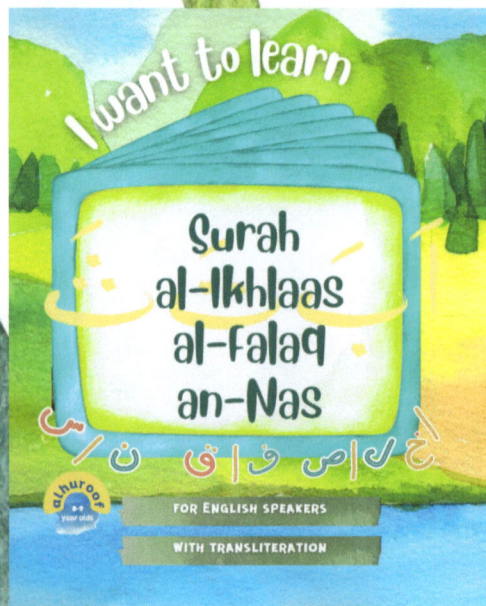

I want to learn

الفاتحة
Surah
al-fatihah

FOR ENGLISH SPEAKERS

I want to learn

Surah
al-Ikhlaas
al-Falaq
an-Nas

FOR ENGLISH SPEAKERS

I want to learn

الفاتحة
Surah
al-fatihah

FOR ENGLISH SPEAKERS

WITH TRANSLITERATION

I want to learn

Surah
al-Ikhlaas
al-Falaq
an-Nas

FOR ENGLISH SPEAKERS

WITH TRANSLITERATION

designed for young or new Muslims

Arabic and Engish

meaning or meaning with transliteration

word by word

ayah by ayah

whole surah

Al Huroof Publishing

www.ingramcontent.com/pod-product-compliance
Lightning Source LLC
Chambersburg PA
CBHW042006080426

42733CB00003B/25